AWESOME ATHLETES

SHAQUILLE O'NEAL

Paul Joseph
ABDO & Daughters

Published by Abdo & Daughters, 4940 Viking Drive, Suite 622, Edina, Minnesota 55435.

Copyright © 1997 by Abdo Consulting Group, Inc., Pentagon Tower, P.O. Box 36036, Minneapolis, Minnesota 55435 USA. International copyrights reserved in all countries. No part of this book may be reproduced in any form without written permission from the publisher.

Printed in the United States.

Cover and Interior Photo credits: Wide World Photos
                                    Allsport USA

Edited by Kal Gronvall

Library of Congress Cataloging-in-Publication Data

Joseph, Paul, 1970-
Shaquille O'Neal / Paul Joseph.
      p. cm. — (Awesome athletes)
Includes index.
Summary: Traces the development of a young basketball star, who also has a clothing line, owns restaurants, has been in movies, made rap albums, has his own record label, and has a business empire worth many millions.
ISBN 1-56239-642-0
1. O'Neal, Shaquille—Juvenile literature. 2. Basketball players--United States—Biography—Juvenile literature. [1. O'Neal, Shaquille. 2. Basketball players.] I. Title. II . Series.
GV884.054J67 1997
796.323'092—dc20
[B]   96-25155
                                                        CIP
                                                        AC

Contents

The Shaq Attack

No one in the game of basketball has added as much excitement and fanfare as Shaquille O'Neal. The **National Basketball Association (NBA)** waited patiently while the Shaq played college ball. After three years of college, O'Neal decided it was time to try the NBA.

He not only gave it a try—the Shaq attacked it—bending rims and shattering backboards with his thunderous dunks on his way to the **Rookie of the Year** Award.

The 7-foot-1-inch, 303-pound O'Neal was the first player chosen in the 1992 NBA **draft**. In fact, when the NBA held the **lottery** to see who would get the first pick in that draft, most referred to it as the Shaquille O'Neal lottery. Every team in the lottery had a team jersey with O'Neal's name and number on it, in hopes of winning the lottery and getting the Shaq.

The lucky team was the Orlando Magic. The Magic immediately signed O'Neal to the richest **contract** in NBA history—$41 million over seven years!

Shaquille quickly showed that he was worth it. He not only packed the house in Orlando, but he also sold out every **arena** he visited. Wherever he traveled, fans tried to get an autograph, touch him, or just get a glimpse. He was by far the hottest attraction in the **NBA**.

On the court he dominated the game, leading the league in scoring and becoming an **All-Star**. In his second year he led his team to the **playoffs**. In his third year Shaq and the Magic were Eastern Conference Champions and runners-up in the NBA.

Although Shaquille is one of the best in the game, his success didn't happen overnight. He worked very hard, had a great upbringing, was disciplined, and stayed out of trouble.

Shaquille is drafted by the Orlando Magic.

Little Warrior

Shaquille O'Neal was born on March 6, 1972, in Newark, New Jersey, to a single mother named Lucille O'Neal. Lucille wanted her son to be somebody special and gave him the Islamic name Shaquille Rashaun. In Arabic, Shaquille means "little one" and Rashaun means "warrior."

Shaquille was never a little warrior. He was a big warrior. Shaq was always much bigger than other kids his age.

Lucille struggled financially to take care of her son. But she made sure that he had everything he needed by working two and sometimes three jobs.

Lucille married Philip Harrison when Shaquille was two. Although he wasn't Shaquille's **biological** father, Shaq would always and forever refer to him as his "real" father.

Philip and Lucille wanted the best for their son. Living in the **projects** with all the gangs and drugs was not the place to raise children. So Philip decided he would join the **army** and raise his family on a military base.

Having a father in the army wasn't easy on Shaq because the family moved from base to base. Sometimes Shaquille's family would move two or three times in one year. They lived in almost every region of the United States and even had a stint in **Germany**.

Although Shaquille didn't like the fact that he had to move so much and start all over with new schools and new friends, it did make for a very close family. Shaquille has two younger sisters, Lateefah and Ayesha, and one younger brother, Jamal.

Shaquille's life was lonely at times, but he could always count on two things to cheer him up: his family and basketball.

Picking Up a Basketball

Shaquille and his family moved around so much that he never had any true roots. Because he was always bigger than the other kids, and was always the "new kid on the block," Shaq would sometimes have to do daring things to get some attention. Sometimes it would get him into trouble, such as when he set off fire alarms.

But all of his attention-getters stopped when his father found out. His father, now a **sergeant** in the **army**, disciplined him and kept him in line. But mainly, his dad was there to encourage him to use his talents to better himself.

Shaq's father would encourage him to do two things: to work hard in school and to play sports. His dad would coach him in football, baseball, and basketball. Although

Shaquille was talented in all three sports, it was basketball that he loved.

His father always practiced with his son, teaching him the **fundamentals** of the game over and over. His dad was also a big man who played basketball in college so he knew what Shaquille needed to learn to be a good ball player.

Shaquille wanted to be the best at basketball. But because he grew so fast he tended to be clumsy. Even though he was clumsy, that didn't slow down Shaq. He just worked harder.

He started becoming a star in basketball when his father moved the family to an **army** base in **Germany**. Although Shaq didn't want to move to Germany, he knew he had no choice.

Moving to Germany

While in **Germany**, Shaq worked on his basketball skills. He wanted to improve his jumping ability, so he sought the advice of Dale Brown, a United States college coach, who was hosting a basketball clinic for U. S. **army** soldiers.

Brown was the well-respected basketball coach of Louisiana State University (LSU). Shaq knew full-well how great of a coach Brown was and asked him how he could improve his jumping ability.

Brown responded, "How long have you been in the army, soldier?" Shaq answered, "I'm not in the army, I'm only 13!"

Brown was shocked. He couldn't believe the size and ability this youngster had. By this time Shaquille was 6'5" and dominated players three and four years older than he was.

Brown saw the size of Shaq's hands and feet and knew that he wasn't done growing. He immediately gave Shaq a weight-training schedule and hoped someday that he would be able to coach him in college.

By the time Shaquille was 16, he had become the best high school basketball player in **Germany**. People would come from all over to watch him. He was averaging 18 points and 12 **rebounds** per game.

Shaquille's coach, Ford McMurty, taught him a lot about the game. They had a very special relationship. Since McMurty was just out of college. He was just like an older brother to Shaq.

McMurty remembers Shaq as a hard worker. "He played hard in practice. He was always on time. When you taught him something, you could see him soaking it up."

His hard work paid off. He led his team in almost all categories and carried them into the **playoffs**. Unfortunately, it all came to an abrupt end.

Shaquille had made many friends in **Germany**, and was having fun, enjoying school, and dominating basketball. Then his father was transferred again—back to the United States.

After the first playoff game win, Shaquille was done with basketball in Germany. The plane was leaving for the United States that evening. In the locker room after the game Shaq was dressed and ready to leave. He came up to his coach and said in a choking voice, "Thank you for everything."

Coach McMurty put his arms around O'Neal and hugged him. "He held me so tight," McMurty said. "I could feel his tears dripping on me."

"Coach, I love you," Shaq said. Shaq walked out of the locker room and headed for the airplane which would take him to his new home, San Antonio, Texas.

High School Sensation

When Shaquille walked through the doors of Cole High School in San Antonio, there was cause for excitement. After seeing Shaq, almost everyone asked if he played basketball.

Shaquille came to Cole as a junior and wore a size 17 shoe. By the time he was a senior he shot up to nearly seven feet and his shoe size to a size 20!

Dave Madura was Shaquille's new coach at Cole. Madura had coached the game for many years and had seen many great basketball players, but no one even came close to Shaquille.

Madura remembers that although Shaquille was an awesome basketball player the best things about Shaq were his attitude and his work ethic. "He was hard-working, disciplined, respected authority, and always had a smile on his face," Madura said.

Shaq would often show up one to two hours before practice was scheduled to start, and he was always the last one to leave.

He loved basketball and worked hard at it, but he also loved school. Shaquille got good grades in high school and was well liked by all of his teachers because of his work ethic and his excellent manners. His mother and father made sure that school came first, and Shaquille agreed.

On the court O'Neal led his team to the **playoffs** in his junior year, only to lose in the second round. Shaq was determined to come back his senior year and win the state championship.

Over the summer Shaquille got on another weight training schedule and really bulked up. He dominated the summer league in which he played. Many sporting reports had him ranked the best high school player in the nation coming into his senior year, and he proved them right.

Opposite page: Shaquille O'Neal at Cole High School.

In his senior year, Shaq led Cole High School to a 34-game undefeated season! In every town he played, people would come to see Shaquille. In most gyms there was standing room only, and many times people had to be turned away. People wanted to see this awesome player dominate games, dunk the basketball, swat away opponents' shots, and bend rims with his brute force.

Shaquille led his team in scoring with a 31-point average as he carried them to the state tournament. But that wasn't enough for Shaq—he wanted his team to be the Texas State Champions.

They cruised through to the Championship game behind Shaquille. But in that contest, they met a tough team in Clarksville High School.

The first half was a seesaw battle with four lead changes and a 32-32 tie at halftime. Cole had a nine-point lead at the beginning of the fourth quarter when disaster struck. O'Neal picked up his third and fourth **foul** in a two-minute span—one more and he would be out of the game.

Madura pulled his big man out of the game to save him for the end. But without the Shaq, Cole squandered the lead. With five minutes left in the game Cole only had a one-point lead. Madura sent Shaq back in the game.

Shaquille came in and led the team to an 8-0 run and Cole's first State Championship! After seeing Shaquille dominate the state tournament, many college coaches wanted the Shaq to play at their school. But Shaq already had signed a **letter of intent** with LSU before his senior season started. In fact, he had actually made his decision where to play college ball many years before that.

Shaquille O'Neal during his days at Cole High School.

1972	1985	1989	1991
Born March 6 in Newark, New Jersey.	Moves to Germany where he becomes the best player in the country.	Moves to San Antonio; leads Cole High School to the Texas state championship.	College Player of the Year at LSU.

How Awesome Is He?

Here's how Shaquille's rookie season stacked up against some of the game's greatest centers in their first year:

PLAYER	GAMES	FG%	FT%	REB.	PPG.
Shaquille O'Neal	**81**	**56.2**	**59.2**	**13.9**	**23.4**
Kareem Abdul-Jabbar	82	51.8	65.3	14.5	28.8
Wilt Chamberlain	72	46.1	58.2	27.0	37.6
Patrick Ewing	50	47.4	73.9	9.0	20.0
Hakeem Olajuwon	82	53.8	61.3	11.9	20.6
David Robinson	82	53.1	73.2	12.0	24.3
Bill Russell	48	42.7	49.2	19.6	14.7

SHAQUILLE O'NEAL

TEAM: ORLANDO MAGIC/
LOS ANGELES LAKERS
NUMBER: 32
POSITION: CENTER
HEIGHT: 7 FEET 1 INCH
WEIGHT: 303 LBS.

1992	1993	1994	1996
Signs with the NBA's Orlando Magic.	Wins the NBA Rookie of the Year Award.	Leads the NBA in field goal percentage.	Signs a $121 million contract with the Los Angeles Lakers; helps the U.S. basketball team win a gold medal at the Atlanta Summer Olympic Games.

- **1991 College Player of the Year**
- **1993 NBA Rookie of the Year**
- **1994 NBA Field Goal Percentage Leader**
- **5-Time NBA All-Star Selection**

Highlights

LSU Bound

After helping Shaquille in **Germany** at the basketball clinic, Dale Brown knew that Shaq would be a star. He kept in touch with Shaquille and his family as the years went by. Selecting a college was an easy choice for Shaquille. He would attend LSU and play for Dale Brown.

As a freshman in 1989, Shaquille tried to learn the more difficult college game. He split time with another **center** and got into plenty of **foul** trouble.

In his sophomore year, Shaquille dominated college basketball. He led the nation in **rebounds** and averaged a whopping 27 points per game. For that he was named **College Player of the Year**.

But the team didn't live up to its expectations. LSU had a very talented basketball team but was knocked out in the second round of the **NCAA** tournament.

The following year, basketball fans everywhere knew who Shaquille O'Neal was. He dominated every facet of

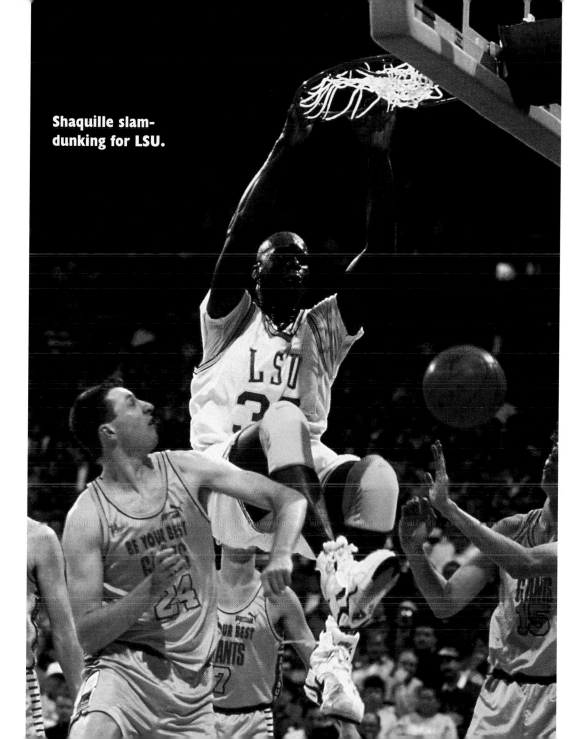

Shaquille slam-dunking for LSU.

the game. Opponents had to change their strategies just because of the Shaq. Sometimes other teams purposely **fouled** him so he couldn't shoot.

Shaquille finished with another awesome season. He was second in the nation in **rebounds** and had a 24-point average. In the second round of the **NCAA** tournament, O'Neal finished the game with 36 points, 12 rebounds, and 5 blocked shots. But LSU lost 89-79. It was Shaquille's last college game.

Although education meant a lot to Shaquille, he knew he could be injured and risk a professional career if he played another college season. Both his parents and Coach Brown agreed with his decision. After three years at LSU, Shaquille decided to turn professional. Everyone knew that he would be the **NBA's** number one **draft** pick.

Shaquille Signs a Deal

It was **lottery** day in the **NBA**, and the future of 11 teams was waiting in an envelope. A team is eligible for the lottery if they did not make the **playoffs** in the prior season.

All 11 teams were represented at the "Shaquille lottery." Each team had prepared a jersey with Shaquille's name and number on it in hopes of hitting the "Shaqpot."

All of the envelopes were opened except for two. It came down to the Charlotte Hornets and the Orlando Magic. "The second pick in the 1992 NBA **draft**," **Commissioner** David Stern said after opening the envelope, "belongs to the Charlotte Hornets."

The last envelope belonged to the Orlando Magic. They had the rights to Shaquille O'Neal! Everyone knew he would be good—but no one had any idea that he would make the awesome impact that he did.

Orlando's **general manager**, Pat Williams, worked 15 solid days until he signed O'Neal to a deal. The final deal was a seven-year **contract** for $41 million.

Shaquille proved he was worth the money with a great **rookie** season. Behind his 23 points per game and a 56 percent **field goal** average, the Magic improved dramatically. Shaquille was named the starting **center** in the **All-Star game** and finished the season with the **Rookie of the Year** Award.

Top pick Shaquille O'Neal drafted by the Orlando Magic.

Orlando's best season before Shaquille showed up was only 31 wins. By Shaq's second year the team was already in the **playoffs**. Although Orlando lost in the first round it was only the start for Shaquille and the Magic.

Eastern Conference Champions

In only Shaquille's third year he had led his team to the **NBA** Championship. The Magic won 57 regular season games— behind Shaq's league-leading 29 points per game average.

In the NBA **playoffs**, the Magic raced to the Eastern Conference title, beating the Boston Celtics, Chicago Bulls, and the Indiana Pacers. The Magic were headed to the NBA Finals to meet the defending champion Houston Rockets.

In the NBA finals the Magic showed their inexperience, losing four games to none. The Magic played hard, but lost two close games by a combined total of five points. Shaquille proved he was ready for the big-time, leading his team with a 28-point average in the NBA Finals.

The Orlando fans were happy with what their team had accomplished so far. And the players knew that they were young and could improve if they worked hard.

Shaquille (left) shows his Olympic medal to teammate Gary Payton.

The next year, in the 1995-1996 season, Shaquille again led his team to an Atlantic division title. And again they raced to the Eastern conference championship. This time though, they met Michael Jordan and the Chicago Bulls, who had won a record 72 regular season games. The Bulls dominated the series, sweeping the Magic in four straight.

Shaq did, however, reach one of his goals. His summer was highlighted by winning an Olympic gold medal. He represented the United States in the 1996 Summer Games in Atlanta.

A Bright Future

Along with Michael Jordan, the Shaq is the best-known player in the game. Shaquille's main goal is to win an **NBA** championship. And because of his work ethic and determination it is a sure bet that he will.

Shaquille O'Neal with the Los Angeles Lakers.

But now he is going to try and win a championship with the Los Angeles Lakers. After four years with the Magic, Shaq had a clause in his **contract** that said he could sign with any team. The Lakers signed Shaquille to the richest contract in NBA history, $121 million over seven years!

"Change is good," O'Neal said. "I'm a military child, so I'm used to relocating. I'm going to miss the children, the fans and the community of Orlando." And it is safe to say the fans of Orlando are going to miss Shaq.

Shaquille also has many other talents to fall back on when his basketball career is over. Because he worked hard in school, Shaquille is very smart and has a business empire, over which he keeps a watchful eye.

Shaquille O'Neal performs with his rap group during the Arsenio Hall Show.

Shaquille has **lucrative endorsement** deals. He has his own clothing line, he owns many restaurants, he has been in two movies, has made three rap albums, has his own record label, and has a host of Shaq-trademarked drinks, snacks, and toys.

His empire is worth millions and millions of dollars. But Shaquille gives his money and time to various **charities**. His main focus is on kids and making sure they have a chance in life.

Shaq's work ethic and determination were instilled in him by his parents, with whom he talks nearly every day. When his mother named him the "Little Warrior," she certainly had the Warrior part right.

Glossary

All-Star - A player who is voted by fans as the best player at one position in a given year.

All-Star Game - A game played at the halfway point of the season between the best players from the Eastern and Western conference.

arena - The building where NBA teams play their games.

army - A branch of the military that has soldiers trained and prepared in case of war.

biological - A direct relation by blood rather than adoption or marriage.

center - an offensive player who plays in the middle, closest to the basket. The center is usually the tallest on the team.

charities - A fund or organization for helping the poor, the sick, and the helpless.

College Player of the Year - An award given to the best college basketball player in the nation.

commissioner - The person in charge of the NBA.

contract - A legal document signed by players that states how much money they will get paid and how many years they will play for a particular team.

draft - An event held where NBA teams choose amateur players to be on their team. After the lottery teams pick, it then goes according to team record with the best getting the last pick.

endorsement - Giving your name and image for money to sell a product.

field goal - When a player shoots and makes a basket. The shot is worth two or three points depending on the distance the shot was made from.

foul - When a player does something against the rules in basketball. A player can get five (six in the NBA) fouls before disqualified from the game.

fundamentals - The basic skills in basketball that are the foundation and the most important.

general manager - The person who runs the overall day-to-day operation of an NBA team.

Germany - A country in central Europe.

letter of intent - A document that student-athletes sign that says they will attend a certain college and play a certain sport.

lottery - An event held in the NBA where teams that didn't make the playoffs get a chance at the first pick in the draft.

lucrative - Making a lot of money and being profitable.

National Basketball Association (NBA) - A professional basketball league in the United States and Canada consisting of the Eastern and Western Conference.

NCAA - This stands for the National Collegiate Athletic Association, which oversees all athletic competition at the college level.

playoffs - Games played by the best teams after the regular season is over to determine a champion.

projects - A group of houses or apartments often built by the government.

rebound - Getting the ball after a missed shot.

rookie - A first-year player in a sport.

Rookie of the Year - An award given to the best rookie player in that particular year.

sergeant - An officer in the army.

Index